Date Due

Memories of Sandy Point
St. George's Bay, Newfoundland

Book editing and design by Joe Blades/Maritimes Arts Projects Productions.

Printed and bound in Canada by Sentinel Printing

Canadian Cataloguing in Publication Data
Pieroway, Phyllis, 1941-

    Memories of Sandy Point, St. George's Bay, Newfoundland

    ISBN 0-921411-33-2

1. Sandy Point (Nfld.) – Social life and customs. I. Pieroway, Charles Warren, 1906-1992. II. Title.

FC 2199.S34A39 1996   971.8   C95-950212-2
F1124.S34P43 1996

Maritimes Arts Projects Productions
Box 596   Ph 506 454·5127
Fredericton NB E3B 5A6   Fax 506 454·5127
Canada   E-mail jblades@nbnet.nb.ca

Memories of Sandy Point
St. George's Bay, Newfoundland

Phyllis Pieroway

from stories told by
Charles Warren Pieroway

Fredericton · Canada

Memories of Sandy Point

Forward

In the mid 1980s I listened intently to a CBC radio interview which gave details surrounding a 1929 offshore earthquake and the devastating waves that washed up on the Newfoundland shores. I had never before asked my parents if they felt the quake on the west coast of the island. Dad's reply made me want to ask questions about the quake and other aspects of their lives.

Dad had been on a coastal schooner in the drydocks in St. John's. They felt the tremor and did not know what it was. But they were to encounter the high waters that swept along the coast: the water came in and marooned them on the deck of the schooner while in the drydock. Not knowing what was happening must have been a frightening experience for everyone. Mother remembered the dishes rattling on the shelves and pictures tilting on the walls in St. George's.

This made me aware of how much I didn't know about life in and around St. George's Bay and especially Sandy Point.

Dad, always known as Charlie, was not one to tell stories. I had to pry details out of him about everyday life experiences. He was the youngest son in a family of five children born to Mary Lorraine (Parsons) and Joseph Henry Pieroway. Dad's brothers had moved to Montreal and his sisters to Toronto so it was his lot to stay at home with his mother. We lived in the family home on Sandy Point until shortly after grandmother died, then the house and property was sold and we moved to Curling, Newfoundland where Dad worked on a scallop dragger owned by Frank Bagg.

Mother had a brother and sister in the Halifax area so she agreed to move to Nova Scotia, but Montreal was to be the final destination. Mother disliked Halifax so much she refused to go any further – if Montreal was ten times bigger then it was going to be ten times more unpleasant. We settled on the Dartmouth side of the harbour.

I had collected pictures from home to add to the chocolate box of treasures mother brought with us to Nova Scotia. One of dad's sisters, Ethel, was an avid photographer who captured images of people and places we now are thankful to have. Putting names to the faces has been difficult as all of dad's family have passed on. One of mother's brothers-in-law, Elwin Berry, his sister Amy (Berry) Martin, and her son Bill, have happily helped me identify some of the people.

Detailed information about the schooners came from the staff of the Fisheries Museum of the Atlantic in Lunenburg, Nova Scotia. A special thanks goes to Ralph Getson, Curator of Education, and Heather Geston.

Thanks also go to Sonia (Pieroway) Comeau for reading the manuscript and giving her input. Without the help of my daughter, Ruth, and son, Joe, this book would never have come together.

Dad's memories are those of a senior, 75-plus. He looked upon everybody and everything in life experiences without criticizing or condemning. He admired the spirit and ingenuity of his fellow ''sand scratchers'' – they did whatever they had to do as best they knew how for all those around them.

When I stand on Sandy Point these days and look around, there is very little to mark the passing of so many people over the low hills and treed fields. The concrete footings that once cradled the magnificent St. Stephen's Anglican Church are overgrown with grasses and trees. Beside it, in the fenced graveyard, I can touch the stones that bear the names of so many of my family. Portions of the old breakwater still stand and the lighthouse still sends its beam out over the harbour waters. Sandy Point is a place of peace and quiet where we ''sand scratchers'' can go and hold a handful of home and watch as it runs through our fingers to scatter on the breeze, just like we have.

– Phyllis Pieroway
Dartmouth, N.S.
October 1995

Sandy Point Map

1. Drawn by Charles Warren Pieroway

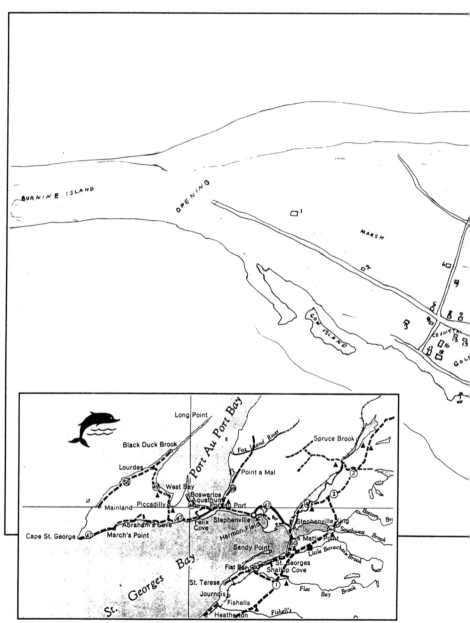

Extract from *Newfoundland Official Road Map 1959* showing Sandy Point, Stephenville Crossing, St. George's Bay, Port au Port...

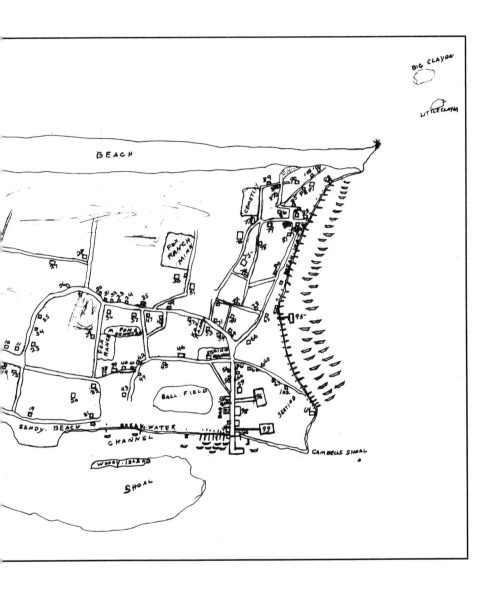

Map Legend

1. Jack Cody
2. George Warren
3. Medrick Sheppard
4. Dave Barry
5. Thomas Younge
6. William Colson
7. Adolph de Basque
8. Clem Lazaga
9. Alfred Lazaga
10. Peter Colson
11. William Colson
12. Jack Younge
13. Henry Halbot
14. Fred Perrier
15. Frances Younge
16. Roman Catholic school
17. Frank Garnier
18. Albert Garnier
19. Joseph Garnier
20. Capt. Hurst
21. Abe Keating
22. Abbey Keating
23. Abe Tilly
24. Man Garnier
25. Sandy Younge
26. Arther Cashin
27. Charles Pennell
28. Jim Younge
29. Max Thomas
30. Alfred Thomas
31. Aleek Messervey
32. George Messervey
33. Joseph Pieroway
34. Reg Berry
35. Frank Swyer
36. Rex Messervey
37. Millage Messervey
38. Frank Pieroway
39. John Renouf
40. Edward Halbot
41. Adolph Halbot
42. Alfred Renouf
43. Brud LeRoux
44. Oliver Alexbnor
45. Son LeRoux
46. William Seward
47. John Messervey
48. William Messervey
49. Daniel McFatridge
50. Charles Vincent
51. Church of England
   ''Protestant'' school
52. Joseph Shaw
53. George Pieroway
54. Wallace Parsons
55. George Boyden
56. Jack Fillman
57. Loyle Boyden
58. Ralph LeRoux
59. Jim Abbot
60. Post Office
61. Niron Messervey
62. Lewis Parsons
63. Walter Swyers
64. Sam Shaw
65. William McFatridge
66. Walter Nicholl
67. Henry McFatridge
68. Sam McFatridge
69. Alfred Pieroway
70. Alfred Messervey
71. Charles Parsons

72. Jim Banfield
73. Joe Banfield
74. Phlip Renouf
75. Jack Renouf
76. St. Stephen's Church of England Parsonage
77. St. Stephen's Church of England
78. Henry Parsons
79. Serg Gooling
80. John E. Parsons
81. Kevin Ralph
82. William Fillatre
83. John Parsons
84. Eddie Parsons
85. Harrold Parsons
86. Bennet Swyer
87. Jim Messervey
88. Jack Parsons
89. Ernest Parsons
90. Gilbert Fillatre
91. George Chin
92. Ulric Chin
93. Sam Hines
94. William Pennell
95. W.H. McFatridge
96. Tavern
97. Barters' Barroom
98. W.H. McFatridge
99. Government Bond Store
100. Smokehouse and mill
101. Salt Storage
102. Bill Hunt
103. Jack Swyers
104. Joe Swyers

Note:

This map was drawn by Charlie Pieroway from memory, many years after Sandy Point had been declared an "outport" by the Newfoundland government in St. John's – when the residents relocated and Sandy Point was abandoned.

It is not known if this map is meant to represent Sandy Point in a specific year in the 1920s-'40s but several known residences have not been illustrated.

Most names listed here are spelled as written on Charlie's original map, or as they appear on gravestones.

A facsimile *Sandy Point Map* is available as an 11" x 14" poster print. Please see pg. 104 of this book.

Playing on the Wharf

I spent a lot of time just playing around the water. I was about 10 when my brothers decided I should learn to swim so they threw me off the end of the government wharf. I had fooled around in the water but it was real deep off the end of the wharf. I sputtered and splashed my way back to the shore. I guess I knew they wouldn't let me come to any harm but I was not pleased. Once I got the hang of it, I was in the water all the time.

One of the things we loved to do was catch sculpins, the swell bellied ones were the kind we most wanted. I think the proper name was a green sculpin.

They weren't easy to catch but when we did get one that's when the fun began. We would take a stick and turn the fearsome-looking creature on it's back and gently tap it on the belly. As the green-coloured sculpin's belly began to swell we would start laughing and hit it some more. When the belly got as big as we wanted it to be then we would place the lumpy thing on it's back in the water. By this time there was so much air in its belly the sculpin could not sink to the bottom, it was completely helpless. What a time we would have. One sculpin was good for at least an hour's hooting and hollering.

There it would lay on the surface of the water with its belly like a balloon and it's eyes bulging out, wriggling its bony tail like mad pushing itself all over the water. Sometimes we would stand on the wharf and try to sink it with stones just to see it pop back up to the surface.

The best times were when several would be caught at the same time, then we were in for a lot of fun. We would lay them all on the stage and start beating on the slimy bellies to see who could get the biggest one. When we had them in the water we could push them under with the stick just to watch them shoot back up, sometimes right out of the water. That was the joy of being a kid in those days.

Nobody ever told us not to do it. The sculpin was so ugly we could pretend they were anybody. They could become your teacher and anybody you wanted to beat up on. It was a good way to vent your anger.

We would catch everything we could around the stages and wharves. We didn't need much to amuse ourselves.

2. School slate and *The Royal Readers, No. 4.*

School

The Church of England schools were in one big building divided into two sections. The lower school took from primer to grade five. The teachers for the little ones were always women.

I remember one, Miss Morgan. She wasn't very big but she had a terrible temper, a real spitfire. We had lots of fun tormenting her. We would put all sorts of things on her chair, in her desk or her coat pocket. Mice always got her dander up. It's too bad we didn't have snakes, they sure would have been useful.

We were sent to the headmaster for strapping. He was a real mean man. Strict! Oh, was he strict. He had a huge leather strap that he used on everyone who didn't toe the mark. Boys and girls got the same treatment. We couldn't get away with anything but that didn't stop us from trying.

Freddie Messervey, Gordie Parsons and a bunch of us used to run away from school. We would go to the woods and play around chasing birds. If we wanted a day off, one of us would

3. The Church of England School.

go to the school at night and stuff a brin bag in the stovepipe. There was a ladder to the roof for safety and chimney cleaning, that made our access of the roof easy. When the fire was lit in the morning, the school would fill full of smoke and we would all be sent home.

The stove was started with kindling but we burned coal. We all had to take turns, one week at a time, tending the stove. We would split the kindling in the evening and go to school real early, 7:30, to get the fire started and the room warm by the time classes opened at 9.

The school was warm, it was built good. It had a big high ceiling with a bell-shaped roof and high arches inside. The stove had to put out a lot of heat to keep it warm. Along one wall there were hooks to hang our wet mittens on. We were not allowed to put them near the stove.

Mr. Eustice was the headmaster. He was a hard man. When it came time to move up into the higher school, 12 of us were to go together. I was the only one who would get to go. The rest went back for three more months in the lower school. They could do that to the kids once. Eustice was so strict. He treated some of the children real bad. He never bothered me much.

Once Charlie Goodland got in trouble over something and Eustice kicked him. Charlie was a big raw-boned guy, about as big as the headmaster. He didn't like being kicked so he kicked back, almost knocked Eustice out. Charlie was suspended for two weeks – he was everybody's hero. We all wanted to do something to the headmaster. Eustice never kicked Charlie again.

One kind man we had as a teacher was Mr. Ward. I don't think he ever strapped anybody. We still gave him a little trouble though. He smoked a big crooked pipe. He carried his plug of Beaver tobacco in his overcoat pocket. Freddie and I used to take it and make cigarettes out of the tobacco. All he ever said was, ''Now, you know, you boys should not do that.'' We liked him a lot. We learned a lot from him.

Every day we began with prayers and then we had to sing *God Save the King*. There was an organ in the school but we would bring the piano over from the parsonage for concerts. A bunch of the boys would load the piano on a sled or cart and move it to the school. We would have had to leave Sandy Point for good if we had damaged that piano. It wasn't easy. There wasn't any place to hold on to and that piano weighed nearly a thousand pounds. We took real good care of it.

The concerts were fun. We would practice in the evenings. We didn't have to take part but almost everybody did. We had a concert at Christmas and another in the spring after Easter. We also had a picnic at the end of the year.

We studied history, geography, math, geometry, literature, grammar and French. I took French for two years. Our exams came out from St. John's. We would write them and send them back. It was well along in the summer before we would get the marks back. That was alright. We never studied any sciences.

The school system went from primary to preliminary to junior then into matriculation and finally intermediate. I think that was about grade 11. I was out when I was 16. If anybody wanted to go on, they went to St. John's. A few girls went, especially if they wanted to teach or be a nurse.

The old school was torn down some years after I finished, as it was very old and hard to keep up. They built a small one-room building in its place. There were fewer people living on Sandy Point by that time so they didn't need a large building.

4. The Goodland house to the right of St. Stephen's church.

Special Days

Lent

There was a church service held every day. All the
children had to go to church every Wednesday and Friday even
if they didn't want to, there was no choice. We also had to go
to church on Sunday as well as Sunday School. During Lent
we weren't allowed to have parties, dances or play cards. I
didn't care for that much but it was no use to complain.

St. George's Day

We would go to school and about ten o'clock the minister
would come and hand out suckers to everybody. They then
gave us the rest of the day off. It was sometime in June, I think
[April 23rd]. I don't remember why it was special but every
day we had off was to our liking.

24th of May

It was called the Queen's Birthday even though the King
was ruling. Everybody had the day off. There was a supper and
dance at the Orange Lodge every year, our family always took
part in all those special times. The Royal Family was real
important to the people. Most houses had a picture of Queen
Victoria, or some of the other members of the family, hanging
in the parlour.

Guy Fawkes Day

In preparation for Guy Fawkes Day [November 5th] we
would go around to all the merchants and gather up all the tar
barrels. They would be glad to get rid of them. The barrels
were made of hardwood and were coated with tar on the inside
so they burned real good. We would pile them, a whole years
supply, out in the middle of the field where we played football.

Sometimes the pile was as high as a house. It took a lot of
work to lift those barrels into place, it was fun though. We
always had a good time when we were doing things like that.

We would all light the pile at the same time. The fire would give off a lot of heat, we couldn't stay near it.

We could see the bonfires in St. George's and Stephenville Crossing. We wouldn't get home until three or four in the morning. It was a Protestant celebration but some of the Catholic kids joined us in our celebration. The first bonfire I went to, I was probably nine years old. We celebrated until we were about sixteen or seventeen or when we went to work.

Old Christmas

We celebrated the full twelve days of Christmas. All the decorations were left up until at least January 6. Nobody worked on Old Christmas Day. It was a day of fun.

We hung our stockings again, just like Christmas Eve. We had big white wool socks, the ones we wore in our logans. They went to our knees – so they could hold a lot of goodies. We always got oranges, apples, candy and nuts. Sometimes there would be a scarf, a pair of mittens or a hat knit by a member of the family.

Old Christmas Day was more fun than Christmas for the young ones because we didn't have to go to church. Dinner was usually goose, beef, or sometimes rabbit with all the trimmings. We usually topped the dinner off with a boiled duff and brown sugar sauce – I still like that the best.

After dinner, we would visit our friends and relatives. Sometimes there would be 12 or 14 of us together going from house to house. Everywhere we visited we had to eat and have a drink. There was lots of parties and dances to go to, a good time everywhere.

If New Year's or Old Christmas fell on Sunday there were no dances. The celebrating was postponed for a day. Nobody ever danced on Sunday.

The Orange Lodge always had a big party. We never got home until the early hours of the next day. The practice of Old Christmas died out around the time of World War II. It was so much fun it seems a shame it isn't celebrated now.

St. Stephen's Churches

The day the old church burned, we were in school. It was in the spring, during Lent, I think. There had been communion in the early morning. We were all let out of school. The bucket brigade couldn't do much to save the building.

They did save some of the articles inside. One piece was a magnificent handcarved wooden Bible stand. It had been donated to the church by Jessie Vincent in memory of Charlie. The stand was an eagle with fully-spread wings. The head and feathers were carved in detail. It was so beautiful. When I had to go to church it was the one thing I liked to look at. I believe some of the linens and silver were saved as well. I was only about seven so things like that weren't important to me then, I didn't pay a lot of attention to what was saved. The actual fire was the big event.

The new church was under construction at the time of the fire. The congregation was big and the old church could hardly hold them all. The silver bell in the old church melted and came down with a great crash. The metal was saved and made into jewellery to raise money for the new bell.

5. [Old] St. Stephen's. Church of England Christmas card.

The logs for the new church were cut up Flat Bay or behind St. George's. They were sawed at Butt's in St. George's or Coulsons on Sandy Point. They were hauled to the site by horse and cart. There was a lot of loads. They built a big church.

I can remember seeing the blueprints. We kids spent a lot of time there doing anything we could. The window frames were made at Halbolts & Colsons. The stained glass windows came by schooner from St. John's. They were probably made in England. They were all dedicated windows, the people were generous and helped in many ways. A lot of the furnishings and materials were donated as well.

The women held parties, hot suppers and picnics to raise money. All the construction was done by local people. It was a magnificent building with a great high steeple.

The new bell was raised in the tower by using several sets of block and tackle. When the bell was lifted into place the floor was built under the frame the bell rested in.

We all used to take turns trying to ring the bell. That was fun. It was hard to get it moving in the cold of the winter. The grease was thick and it took a lot of pulling to start it moving. Sometimes we pulled it so hard the bell turned over. We

6. St. Stephen's New Church. 1916 Christmas card.

weren't supposed to do that. The bell made a glorious sound when it was properly rung.

The church had big brass lamps hanging from the arched rafters. The wires were put on the hooks from the scaffolding. Each lamp had four fine chains so we could pull them down to light them then raise them back in place. They had to be kept polished. They were beautiful lamps.

The interior was all finished by hand – hardwood panelling all sanded and shellacked. Everything was painted and polished for the dedication in the summer. That was one service I didn't mind going to. The bishop came and a lot of ministers were there also. As far as I know, the new St. Stephen's was completely paid for by the time it opened.

The furnishings were brought in by schooner from St. John's. They were probably built in England or the States.

7. Cornerstone dated 1913 for the "new" St. Stephen's Church. Photo taken in 1992.

The *Arnish*

She was built in 1917 in a yard at the mouth of Barachois Brook, on the western side. She was a three-master, the biggest ship I saw built around home.

I was 11 when she was built. They launched her in the spring. Everybody from around Bay St. George went to the big event. Boatloads of people were anchored off the slipway. We were all let out of school for the day.

The ship was christened by a lady, a relative or member of the builder's family, I think. Champagne was used to christen her, as was usual for that sort of occasion. The *Arnish* didn't launch the first time they tried. She stuck on the slipway. She moved about the length of herself than stopped dead. The old folks there talked of a bad omen when a ship does not launch properly.

Two weeks later, on a Saturday, she slipped down the way. She was painted white with black tops on the rails. The minister blessed the ship and the champagne was broken again. The ladies were all dressed in their finest. It was quite a sight. The owners came from St. John's for the launch.

She was manned by a crew from all over the island. After the launch, they tied her up at the government wharf. The three spars were brought in on a boat. I spent many hours watching the crew putting the masts and rigging in place. The canvas was a white as the snow and a lot of it.

The day she sailed out of the harbour, we all went out on the back of the beach to watch her leave. That was a beautiful sight with all the sails set. We never saw her again. She sank on her maiden voyage.

She was loaded with lumber. They found her still afloat. The crew all got off safe. We heard that they towed her into port somewhere in the States and turned her into a steamboat. I don't know if that is true or not. Of course, she didn't really sink, since she was loaded with lumber. I guess the old folks were right.

Schr: "Arnish"
Reg. No: 142106 (Registered 11 Sept. 1919)
Built: 1917
Built by: Fleet & Aulk, St. George's, Nfld.
Length: 140'5"   Breadth: 31'2"   Depth: 14'6"
Reg. tons: 466.64   Signal Letters
Gross tons: —   T
                             C
                             R
                             B
Master:
Owners: Joseph Fleet of St. George's, Nfld., Merchant.
Transactions:
Joseph Fleet sold vessel 12 Sept. 1919 to Arnish Shipping
Co., St. John's, Nfld.
Registry closed 28 May 1920; vessel totally lost 120 miles
E. by N. from Fogo, Nfld., on 2 November 1919.

St. John's Shipping Register - Reel #C 4850
Fisheries Museum of the Atlantic, Lunenburg, N.S.

[As she was built in 1917 but did not sink until 1919 it is possible she was not on her maiden voyage, as Charlie said, or she was considered to have "sunk" twice.]

The Royal Navy in St. George's Bay

There was a golf course on Sandy Point when I was a young
fellow. The British Navy built the golf course, it was up near
the Catholic School on the harbour side. Every summer,
shortly after the navy ships arrived, about 30 men were
brought ashore to clean up the area and make it ready for play.

We always looked forward to them arriving. The officers
dressed in whites: shoes, knee socks and knee-length shorts.
We carried their golf bags while they played. That was a lot of
fun – not really work. We got paid but we also got to keep all
the balls we found outside the course. We used them when the
sailors weren't around. We had a lot of good times playing
around on the golf course.

The ships would come in five or six times during the
summer. The population of Sandy Point and St. George's grew
quickly when they were all in port. It was the only times we
ever had any mass of visitors. They were there for rest and
relaxation. They always had a good time. After World War I,
they came in more often than before and there were more ships
in the fleet as well.

The launch brought the sailors ashore. And on Sunday
afternoons we could go on board. We were taken on guided
tours of the ships. They explained everything to us. We asked
lots of questions.

When I was about 16, they took a bunch of us out for a
day on one of the ships. We went out off Cape St. George.
They showed us how they prepared for combat. That was an
interesting day for all of us. They always had lots of food on
board.

When they were in Bay St. George in August and
September, Dad and I sold them fresh fish. We set a trawl
outside and every day we would haul it and take the fish along
side the ships. The sailors would individually buy the fish they
wanted to cook. They would lower a bucket over the side with
cigarettes, chocolate and money for the fish. We gladly took

the goodies and sent up the fish. They loved flounder. Many times we would sell all we had. When there was a lot of ships in we did real good.

In the evenings, the ship's bands would come on deck and play. We could hear the music all over the harbour on a calm evening. Mother really loved listening to the bands. We would go off to the big ships in our little boats. The people would come from all around the harbour. It was a grand sight to see all those boats on those warm summer evenings. The sound of the music drifting across the water sure was a wonderful sound. I can still remember the fun we had. Everybody looked forward to hearing the bands. Those were happy times.

Fox and Mink Ranches

Loyle Boyden, Edmond Parsons and Charlie Pennell raised mink. Charlie Parsons and Millage Messervey raised fox. Charlie Vincent had both fox and mink at his ranch.

Charlie Vincent had the largest ranch. It was down by the school. The ranch ran back through the woods toward the beach. Charlie worked the ranch and his wife, Jessie, ran the store. All the longhouses were surrounded by a wire fence down about two feet in the sand, so the foxes couldn't dig their way out. Outside the wire fence was a wooden fence about eight feet high to keep out noise. This was especially important when the young mink are being born. When the mink are frightened they kill their young.

Charlie kept many different breeds of mink and fox. Black, patch, silver and red foxes were common. The blue mink was my favourite – so black it looked blue.

Each fox had its own wire pen in the longhouse. The ground under them was sand so there was good drainage all around. The foxes were fed dried fish, herring, skate or dogfish. Cod liver oil was mixed in their food. Charlie had a big building where he made the special bran cakes he fed his animals. There was a big oven in there. Wild meat was used whenever they could get it. They fed a lot of horse meat as well. They would buy the carcass of old horses from all around the area. Anyone who had a horse that was too old or injured was sure to be able to sell it to the fox ranchers after they killed it.

They would kill off from 1,400 to 1,800 foxes each year. The skins were split down the belly and stretched over wooden molds, then stored in a shed to dry. They made all the molds out of boards. Carved them all by hand.

As children, we were allowed to feed the foxes and go around with them as they took care of all the pens. We were never allowed to be around when they killed and skinned the animals. We could go and see the pelts after they were on the stretchers.

Buyers would come every fall from the mainland. They would sell to whomever offered them the most for the pelts. In those days, women wore the full fox. They were done up real nice and a prize to have. They looked real smart with the fox wrapped around their shoulders.

The mink were fed the same as the foxes. We used to weigh out their food. Dad and I sold the ranchers a lot of dry skate, dogfish and herring. The dogfish would get in our salmon nets – they were a nuisance.

We would split the dogfish down the middle, leaving the tail, then hang them on poles to dry. The skate we hung on the fence. The herring were split down the back and laid on flakes. We gathered capelin and dried them for fox food too.

As kids, we had a lot of fun around the ranches. The animals got used to us as we helped carry the food. That was a great way to spend our time.

8. Charlie Parson's House on the left and the Orange Lodge at the far right.

The Orange Lodge

Protestants only joined the Lodge. All members wore their sash and pin. Dad [Joseph Henry Pieroway] was Grand Master for years. They had a lot of rules and regulations. No children or women were permitted to join or attend meetings but the entire family took part in the picnics and special celebrations.

Their special day was July 12. Orangemen's Day. The members would gather at the Lodge and march in a parade to the church for their special service. Then they returned for their own meeting.

Nobody worked that day. Since most of Sandy Point was Protestant, all the stores, post office and businesses closed. Dad never worked that day so I had to haul the nets by myself. Almost everybody went to the picnic after the meeting. A local band played – usually violin, banjo and piano.

Suppers were served upstairs in the Orange Lodge building. It was a big building. Four long tables were set with white linen cloths, silver and china. The food was always fantastic. All the ladies brought their finest creations. Meat was always the main course. Fish, not even lobster, was not a treat as it was always there. We could always bring our own liquor, either the homemade variety or bought from the barroom or bootlegger. We bought our rum in one or two gallon jugs. It came in by boat from St. Pierre and Miquelon.

9. Joseph Henry Pieroway's Orange Lodge pin.

Stores

Nicholle's store was at the end of the boardwalk. They sold groceries. They had a son named Walter, but I can't remember their names.

Walter and Ralph Leroux's store was half-way along the walk. The store was on the front of their house. They sold groceries, clothes, general hardware – just about everything was available there. The stock was brought from Halifax on the Farquhar Line ships – they carried freight and passengers.

Charlie Vincent's store was up by the Protestant School. They had groceries. Later the store was sold to Gordon Tilley.

Loyle Boyden ran a grocery store as well.

McFatridge's store was in their old house. They had their own schooner that brought supplies from Halifax. The store was always well stocked. The first schooner I sailed on, the *MacKenzie*, was theirs.

10. Pitcher bought by Charlie for his mother on his first working voyage.

Pennell's store was down from the church toward the lighthouse. They sold everything you could possibly need.

Bennett Swyers carried groceries and general hardware plus clothes, socks, overalls, mitts and boots. We had a pretty good selection to choose from when I was young.

Fred Perrier had a store in what we called Dog Town – where the Roman Catholics lived. More dogs than people, we were always told. The Protestants and Catholics didn't get along too good – terrible things we used to say and do to each other.

There were no barber shops. We got our hair cut by a couple of local men who did it in their homes.

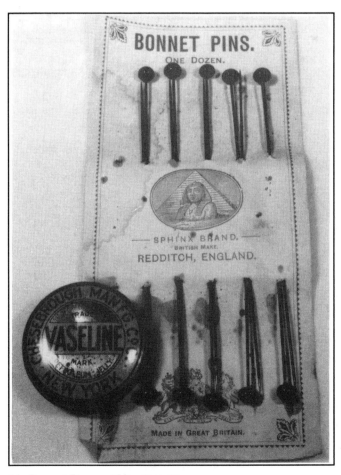

11. Bonnet Pins and Vaseline tin.

Supplies for the Stores

Supplies for the stores came by schooner, until later years when the train would bring goods to St. George's and then they'd come across the harbour by boat or sled.

Molasses came to the stores in 90- or 120-gallon puncheons. We would carry our own crockery jug to the store to draw off a gallon of molasses. There were smaller barrels of 40- or 24-gallons – they were made of oak with iron hoops. Some people bought a small barrel for their family use. Kerosene was sold the same way. Everybody had their own can.

Sugar came in 250-pound barrels. They were heavy and hard to handle. I rolled many a barrel along the wharf to the store. Salt beef, pork, pig's heads and jowls all came in barrels. Flour was packed in 190-pound barrels. Most people bought enough flour to last them the winter. We usually had five or six barrels at home.

Crackers were packed in wooden boxes – five pounds to a box. The cover on the box lifted half way. The boxes were on

12. Parfum Pompeïa from Paris.

the counter where the store owner could keep an eye on them, kids like crackers a lot. Cheese was on the counter as well. The heads of cheese were so good. Every fall we had to buy enough cheese to last us a winter until the ice went out in the spring. We could eat a lot of cheese as it was easy to carry with us in the woods or fishing. Butter was packed in wooden tubs, 20- or 30-pound sizes. The butter came in from Halifax.

Candy: there was lots of candy all the time. A penny would buy a lot. One or two cents was all we ever spent. A real spree might see you spend five cents. You could hardly get it all in your pockets. You certainly couldn't eat it all.

Bolts of cloth of all colours and patterns, ladies' supplies, gloves, hats and all sorts of fancy things were in the stores. Perfume from St. Pierre and Miquelon was on the shelves – nothing but the best. Bottles of medicine, pills, liniments, lotions and all the everyday needs were there.

The stores on Sandy Point were well-stocked when I was a kid and there were lots of people living there.

13. Oriental fan.

Going to Nova Scotia

Along with food, everything needed by the stores and individual people in the area, furniture, all kinds of clothes, many bolts of fabric was brought back on the schooners and coastal boats. Flannelette so thick it was like a blanket. There was always barrels of apples, sugar, flour, meat and molasses on board. The captain and crew would buy anything people wanted special – fancy dishes, jewellery and lots of candy.

I went to Halifax, for the first time, when I was nine. I went on the schooner with Dad. Jack Parsons was the mate. He took me to Dartmouth on the paddlewheel ferry. That was really something to talk about. There wasn't much to Dartmouth then, that would have been 1915. The paddlewheel was fascinating to watch, nothing like that around home.

Another time, we put into the Imperial Oil Refinery on the Dartmouth side of Halifax Harbour for a load of kerosene. They loaded 40 barrels, if I remember correctly. They were loaded on deck so we had to stay there the night. Some of the crew took me with them for a walk on shore. There wasn't much of a road, mostly mud. It was nice to get ashore even for a short time but I loved being on the schooner with the men.

14. Carnival glass sugar bowl.

Canneries

There were 12 or more canneries around St. George's Bay: Cashin, Pennel, Messervey, Shaw, Parsons, Butt, and Pieroway were some of them.

Dad canned lobster and salmon for years. He would boil the lobster, shell them, and pack the claws and tails only. It was packed by weight in one-pound cans. We used scales with weights on one side and the can on the other, we filled the can until it balanced. The cans were then sealed. Next we had to punch a small hole in the lid to let out the steam while it was boiling in the bath. When the cans were out and cold we had to solder the hole to seal it tight.

The bodies were never used – we could eat all we wanted. The kids sure had a feast, as well as the gulls.

We packed the salmon raw. The pieces were cut to fit the can. I think we added a little salt, then we sealed the cans and put them in the boiling bath for about two and one-half hours. We packed one- and two-pound size cans. They were sold to dealers in Halifax and St. John's.

Salmon

One year I ran a smack for Sam Butt. Bob White from St. George's ran the other one. He did one side of the harbour and I did the other. I went to Stephenville, Seal Cove and out to Port au Port.

I can remember seeing Jack Swyers with his big dory full to the top with salmon – the gunnel just barely out of the water. There were lots of fish then. People today can't imagine what it was like.

The smack I ran was big – 34 feet – with a small cabin over the wheel and engine, and the rest of her open. Often we came back loaded – the gunnel about seven inches above the water. The average salmon was 12 to 15 pounds with many 20 to 25 pounds.

The biggest one Dad and I caught weighed 52½ pounds. It was 12-inches thick (down through), 30-inches long and six-inches wide on the back. What a fish!

On Sundays, we would get a bunch together – boys and girls, pack a lunch and go salmon fishing with a rod in the rivers. We would have a great time seeing who could catch the biggest salmon on a line. They were good eating – nothing better.

Killicks

We would take two pieces of spruce about two-feet long and notch each piece in the middle so they would fit together like a cross. Then we had to bore one-inch holes 10 to 12 inches apart. We would then take birch or spruce rods and taper them down so they would fit tightly in the holes. A large rock was put in between the rods. The rods were usually about two-feet long.

Then we had to haul the rods together at the top and wrap them with wire about 20 times. On top of the wire we served it with rope for eight inches so it wouldn't come apart. The rope gave us something to hold on to.

The killicks weren't all that good as they rolled on the bottom. When we were able to get real anchors made, we didn't use killicks very often. Mostly we used them on herring nets, smelt nets and lobster pots. We never used them on salmon nets if we could help it – the nets would get all tangled up when they rolled. What a mess to try to straighten out.

We always had a killick in the boat with 70-fathom of rope on it to use in case the engine quit and we needed to stop drifting.

15. A killick.

Fishing Nets

We would knit two and some years three salmon nets in the winter. We set the net up in the kitchen, everybody knit whenever they had time. The salmon nets were a joy to knit, the mesh was five-inch, so it went along fast. We stuffed it into a sack as we knit to try to keep it out of the way.

We used cotton twine mostly, a few knit hemp in the latter years. We used #15 thread for the lead and #12 for the pound. When it was knit, we mounted it on head ropes. A 20-fathom net was 60-feet long, three to one. We would stretch the new head ropes as much as we could. One head rope was 12-thread and the second 15-thread. The floats fit between the head ropes. The floats were 12-incles long and five wide with a slot in each end so the rope fit in tightly. They were tied in place.

16. Frank Hines repairing nets, Sandy Point.

When the net was all together, we tanned it in a juniper and spruce mixture. We would put the net in the big cast iron pot when the tan was warm and leave it in there for two days. Then the net was taken out and dried. That made the net about the same colour as the water, a brownish colour. The water coming into the harbour out of the rivers was real brown, lots of natural tannin.

Fishing Herring

Herring nets were hateful to knit – the mesh was two inch The net was 120-mesh deep and 60-fathoms long. You could knit for hours and not seem to get anywhere. The herring nets were mounted and tanned the same as the salmon nets.

The herring nets were set straight with an anchor on each end and a buoy as a marker. Sometimes every mesh would have a fish in it. At times, we were just able to haul the net across the boat to shake it. We would say that there were two in the same direction and one in the other direction as a wedge. Our arms would ache. So would all your body by the time we finished hauling. The boat would be full.

When the herring were spawning in the spring we could just barely keep ahead. At times there were so many we would tie up the net for a while until we had handled all we had. If they got in the nets and died we had a job to shake them out.

Getting the herring in the boat was only the beginning. We would take them to our store, load them in wheelbarrows and dump them in tubs to wash them. Then we had to split and clean them before packing them in salt. We had to work fast and steady. It was a lot of hard work for what we got out of it – it was just barely enough to live on.

Packing Fish

When I was about 12, as soon as we were out of school for the day, we went right to packing herring until about eight o'clock. Everybody had to work to get them all split, gutted and packed when the run was on. We had to catch them fast because sometimes they didn't stay around long.

Some women worked at packing. None of our family let the women work in the store. They always brought us hot lunches at about three in the afternoon, we wouldn't get supper until eight or nine, some days.

The herring were shipped to Halifax to Farquhar, Wentzells or Smith Bros. On Sandy Point, we packed about 250,000 to 300,000 barrels every spring.

The herring went to Halifax in schooners and we brought back food and clothes and other needs.

Dad captained a schooner after the herring run ended, from July to Christmas. Sometimes they would bring back salt. They never stopped, they would load with herring and go to Halifax, off-load and take on supplies and return back home as fast as possible. Sometimes they would put into Malagash for salt but most of the time they loaded it in Halifax.

Smelt Fishing

We set our nets in September up at the bottom of Flat Bay by Jaunters Island, Seal Cove, the mouth of Barachois Brook or Flat Bay Brook.

There were 12 to 14 nets on a fleet, one behind the other: six-feet deep and 14-fathoms long. The nets were knit out of cotton linen. The mesh was one and one-half to one and three-quarter inches. There weren't any restrictions on the size of the mesh.

We hauled the nets every morning at daybreak. We would catch a lot. The nets were always full.

In the winter, we fished through the ice. We cut a hole eight-feet long by two-feet wide. We then lowered the trap into the hole. It had a long leader – 100-yards -- and a pound like a salmon net. Iron bars were used for weights to keep the nets on the bottom. We covered the hole with fir boughs to cut out most of the light. We always left a couple of peep holes so we could see the fish as they went into the net. We would haul the net when we figured there was enough fish inside. It wasn't easy if there was a lot of smelts in the net.

One time, Walter Parsons and I had a trap set up by Cow Island, just below the opening. When we hauled the net, it sure was full. We had a hard time getting it out of the water. We had 2,500 pounds. We loaded boxes, four-feet by one-foot high, and Walter took them home with the horse and sleigh. I stayed there and we hauled until we got all of them on shore. We got 20 to 30 cents a pound. We would freeze them and ship them to Sydney, Halifax or New York. Once we got 50 cents a pound – that was real good money. They were shipped by train in freezer cars from St. George's to Port-aux-Basque, across to Sydney and then on to New York.

For fun, almost everybody fished through the ice. We would cut a small hole, bait the hook with sand worms dug up along the shore or with pieces of salt pork. When we caught the first smelt we would cut its throat out and use it as bait. It is real white and shows up good in the water. A piece of red flannel was tied on also to attract the smelts. Children had lots of fun smelt fishing.

When we had a trap down on the bottom, we often got lots of flounder. The iron bar would stir up the mud on the bottom and the flat fish would come up in the net – that was a bonus. Fresh fish in the winter was a treat.

We fished for trout any time of the year. We especially liked fishing in Little River. We only took what we could eat. There was no need to take any more as we could get them whenever we wanted them.

We jigged for squid in August and September. We ate some but most went for bait. There were a lot of squid. They would run ashore so we didn't have to fish them. We just picked them up in buckets along the beach.

In the night, we would take lanterns and walk along the shore in the shallow water. The squid would follow the light and run up on the shore after us. Oh, that was fun.

Lobster Pound

The pound was owned by Maurice Boland. I worked there for two years, I was in charge of the cars. I had seven cars to keep stock in. I shipped from 50- to 60,000 pounds a week. The lobster season ran from April 12 to June 12, if I remember right.

Maurice bought from local fishermen. He had a big boat they ran up the coast to collect the lobsters in. They often brought back 20,000 pounds a day. They were packed in 100-pound boxes. We put all the lobsters in the cars and held them until the boat came from Boston. She was a nice little boat, real fast. She could do 25 knots. It took her one and a half days from Sandy Point to Boston. We shipped 60,000 pounds to a load.

The local fishermen were getting from five to six cents a pound for their catch. I could eat all I wanted. I used to take a brin bag full home whenever I felt like having a feed. I liked the 12-inch ones best.

I was working there when I got married in 1938. We had lobster for our wedding party. We boiled them at home that afternoon. We got married in St. Stephen's Anglican church in the evening, seven o'clock, I think. I took the whole day off after the wedding. It was the end of May and right in the height of the season. I couldn't afford to not be there – they needed me and I needed the money.

When the boat from Boston came in, we would unload all the empty wooden crates they brought back. Once, after they were all out, we found two lobsters in the bottom of the hold. I took them to the captain and we both figured that since they had made the round trip alive we should let them go so we threw them over the side.

There were strict rules about the size of the lobster we could keep. Inspectors and research doctors would come unannounced from St. John's. They came in on the train to St. George's. I can still remember the time the research doctor told me about 12-inch lobsters carrying 50,000 eggs. We never really knew much about what we were catching. Nobody thought about running out of stock. There was so many really big lobsters in those days, nobody would have believed what has happened to them.

One year I was a buyer for Boland. We went along the coast in his big boat. I carried a cash box and paid for everything as we bought it. I would have $5-600 dollars with me when I left each morning. At the end of the day I would tally up the load and give the receipts and leftover cash to the office. At the end of the year I was out 52 cents. Boland laughed at that. He didn't make me pay back the difference.

Sandy Point Lighthouse

The lighthouse was built in 1883 with a steel frame and wood exterior and wooden house. The lamps were the kerosene type – when lit the heat would build up and start the reflectors turning. The light flashed every three seconds. The beam could be seen from Cape St. George at the mouth of the harbour.

Millage Messervey was the light keeper when I was young. He lit the lamps every evening and put them out in the morning. The light was about one and a half miles from his house. In a southeasterly rain storm or a northwest snowstorm it was hard going as the point sticks out in the middle of the harbour. There wasn't any protection from any direction.

The sand kept moving and they had to move the lighthouse further out on the point. It was moved about 100-yards closer to the shore at the point. The water is very deep off there so the light had to be as close to the point as possible.

A crew of men were sent in from St. John's. They built the new base. It is 27-feet above sea level. The lighthouse was moved by using block and tackle, rollers, horses and a lot of men. That was quite an operation, I spent every minute there I could.

There wasn't any wrecks in the area that I can remember. The harbour is so wide there is little danger.

The keeper had to paint the lighthouse every summer – red and white of course. He also received the shipment of kerosene in the summer. It came from St. John's in four-gallon cans. Two cans to a case. The keeper had to handle and store the kerosene. Everything about the lighthouse was totally his responsibility.

Freddie took over the keeper's job from his father when he got old enough. He used his two dogs and the sleigh to travel to and from the light. I had a team of dogs as well. We used to have great fun with them. We used to race to the light. I spent a lot of time with Freddie at the lighthouse.

[The automatic flasher was installed around the time of World War II. The light is 35 feet above high water. The character of the light is flashing white showing 10 flashes of one second duration per minute.]

17. The present-day lighthouse.

On the *J. Henry MacKenzie*

The *MacKenzie* was owned by the McFatridge family. She had been built in Lunenburg by Smith & Rhuland. She was 110-feet in length, 26-in breadth and about 10-feet deep when built. She was registered for just under 100-tons.

I was 17 the first day I went on board. Captain William White told me to go up the main mast to help Jim Parsons to strap the mast head. The main mast was 80-feet! I had to climb the rigging on the outside, I sure was scared. Two days we worked on the mast head. We had to hang on with one hand and work with the other while standing on a one-inch steel cable. After a few times up, it didn't bother me any more. I guess they had to know right away if I could do what they wanted done. I passed the test, they kept me on the crew.

The *MacKenzie* came in second in trials with the *Bluenose*. She was build along the same lines. Her rail would touch the water but never go under. She sure could move.

On one trip to Halifax we had to put into Sydney Harbour to get out of a sou'west gale. It had been blowing for two days. The *John Ford* and another schooner from the south coast came into Sydney after we did. The *Ford* was loaded with fish.

The crews were friends. They challenged each other as to who would put into Halifax first. The wind died down in the evening and we left after dark. We could see the others getting underway so we hustled.

We came inside Scatarie Island with the wind out of the southeast. We ran into black fog, we couldn't see much. We had every bit of sail on. She was cutting through the seas at a nice clip. We passed to the win'ard of the *Ford* about one the next morning. We never saw the other schooner all night. We came into Halifax Harbour about dawn and anchored off George's Island. The *Ford* came in about 9 and the last schooner at 9:45.

We all enjoyed those races. It made getting there more fun than work. Even though we had to work hard it was good most of the time. We had a four-hour watch. We'd get up, dress, eat and stand watch. We would steer for the first hour then one hour on the bow and turn about. When the watch ended, we would wash, eat and, if we were lucky, get two and a half to three hours sleep before we had to stand watch again.

Sometimes we would get real tired. We didn't get much sleep on some of the trips. If someone got sick or hurt we would have to take their turn as well as your own. We had to be so careful in the fog and the driving snow or sleet.

Schr:	"J. Henry MacKenzie"			
Reg.No:	134.045			
Built:	Feb.13, 1914 (launched)			
Built by:	Smith & Rhuland, Lunenburg, N.S.			
Length:	109'8" Breadth: 26'3" Depth: 10'4"			
Reg. tons:	99.73			
Gross tons:	-			
Master:	Archibald Geldert			
Owners:				
M.O. William C. Smith,	Lunenburg	Merchant	11	shares
Archibald Geldert	Lunenburg	Mariner	2	"
Benjamin Smith	"	"	2	"
William Duff	"	Merchant	2	"
Abram Cook	"	Mariner	2	"
Edwin Backman	"	"	2	"
George Myra	"	Rigger	2	"
Clarence Myra	"	Mariner	2	"
Alfred Herman	"	"	2	"
Thomas Walters	"	Blacksmith	2	"
David Heisler	"	Mariner	2	"
Frank Whynacht	"	"	2	"
Moyle Smith	"	Merchant	2	"
Daniel Eisenhauer	"	Machinist	2	"
Alfred Whynacht	"	Farmer	2	"
Maud Young	"	Widow	2	"

Gabriel Emeno	"	Mariner	2	"
Frederick Peterkin	"	Trader	2	"
Dawson Geldert	"	Mariner	2	"
Adelaide Holland	"	Married Woman	2	"
Christian Geldert	"	Mariner	2	"
Reuben Ritcey	Riverport	"	2	"
Daniel McDonald	Pictou	Contractor	3	"
Arthur H. Whitman	Halifax	Merchant	4	"
Allan Goodridge & Sons Ltd., St. John's. Nfld.			4	"

64 Shares

Transactions:

William C. Smith sold 4 shares to J. Henry MacKenzie of Pictou, farmer, Sept. 21, 1914.

J. Henry MacKenzie dies at Bayview, Pictou Co., N.S., Oct. 26, 1914. His executor, Montreal Trust Company, sold his 4 shares to Florence May of Bayview, May 11, 1916.

Shareholders sold out to William H. Smith (of W.C.S.), Merchant, Lunenburg, April 30, 1926.

William H. Smith sold vessel to Henry McFatridge, Merchant, St. George's Bay, Nfld., May 1, 1926.

Ship stranded 13 Oct. 1934*. Registry closed 12 Nov. 1934.
*Vessel stranded Bradore Harbour, Province of Quebec.

Lunenburg Shipping Register
Fisheries Museum of the Atlantic, Lunenburg, N.S.

The Customs House

The Customs House was down by the government wharf. It was a big building with a lot of warehouse space. Everything coming in from Canada, U.S.A. and St. Pierre & Miquelon was stored there. It was run by Joe and Bill Pennell. Abraham Tilley was the customs officer and Ulrich Chin was the tidewaiter.

Not everything passed through customs. It was a real game to get things home without paying the duty. The tidewaiter would come on board when we got in port. If any of us wanted to take things off, the rest of the crew would get Ulrich below deck and give him a drink and start playing cards. While he was below we would load whatever we wanted in a dory on the off side and row for shore. Mostly we did that sort of thing at night.

On one trip to Halifax Fred Parsons had ordered an overcoat from Eaton's. I had it and another overcoat, pants and shoes to get home. We always declared something so they would not suspect us or give us a hard time. Most of what I bought that time didn't have any duty paid on it.

Fishing boats would come in to port from St. Pierre & Miquelon – they always had liquor on board. We would get a couple of gangs together. One to keep the customs officer occupied plus three or four watchmen. The other crew would go out to the boat and get the liquor and bring it back to shore where others would be waiting. We could move it real fast when we had too. I don't know if the customs officer ever caught anybody. Somtimes it took two gangs to keep him busy so we could get all the stuff off the boat. I am sure he knew what we were up to but he never caught us with anything, we sure had a lot of fun those times.

In the schooners they had all sorts of places built in to hide stuff, under the cabin floor and around the rudder casing. On the *MacKenzie* we often hid a lot of goods. The McFatridges had a store in the Crossing as well as in Sandy Point. On one trip we hid four or five cases of shoes under the cabin floor. When we got in port a few of the crew took Ulrich below for the usual game of cards. The rest of the crew got the shoes out, loaded them in a boat and headed for Stephenville Crossing as fast as she would go. Nobody saw them so they got away with it. We would get a pair of shoes for our efforts – they were worth a lot to us in those days.

18. A selection of Newfoundland coins from 1909 to 1943 bearing King Edward VII, then King George V.

Government Wharf and Breakwater

There have been many wharves built over the years. The first ones were straight. Then they built a T on the end. The last time there was a T on the east side. The ice would break the logs and the rock would spill out and everything would have to be put back.

There was always one man in charge of the repairs but anybody could work. We got paid 25 cents an hour in the 1920s for our effort. We mostly picked up rock for the inside.

We would go across to Barachois Brook and take the rock off the shore at the mouth of the river. The water was usually real cold when the work had to be done. We would stand in the water up to our knees and pick or shovel the rock off the bottom and load them in the boat. The big ones we rolled up on the shore on plank and then onto the boat. We then had to take them across the harbour and unload them by hand and put them in the wharf. The weather wasn't always the best but the wharf had to be repaired.

19. The damaged breakwater after a storm.

The breakwater stretched from up near the Catholic School to near the lighthouse on the harbour side of Sandy Point. It was built of timbers spiked together, with rocks piled inside. Most of the breakwater was about eight-feet wide and six- to seven-feet high. The top was boarded over to make a real nice walkway along the shore.

Whenever the breakwater was damaged there was a pile of material on hand to repair it right away. The rock didn't go far so we just had to rebuild the frame and fill it up again. It often broke and the water would spread far across the low areas.

I've seen it almost up to the school and, once, I rowed up to Uncle Alfred's. There was from one to two feet of water all the way. Our house was high enough we never got any water in it but many houses were damaged. We would have to wear hip waders to walk along the roads.

Down by Tilley's store, at Aunt Beete's [Messervey], the houses in that area often flooded. They would move upstairs until the tide went out. Then they could come back down and hope we got the break repaired before the high tide came back in. We would all work at repairing the break while the tide was out.

Everybody who could help did. It was necessary to get the repairs done fast. Sometimes it wasn't nice weather, gales of wind and snow.

The women made hot lunches for the work crews. Hot rum toddies and molasses buns. The buns would have salt pork chopped up in them. There was not enough rum to make anybody drunk but enough to make you feel warm inside. We had to work as hard as possible to get the breakwater back in place before the tide rose again no matter what time of the day it was. I worked many nights in real bad weather to plug the breaks. The ice and the high tides caused most of the troubles.

Telegraph Office and Post Office

The Telegraph Office and the Post Office were in the same building as the Custom's Office. The postmistress was Minnie McFatridge, Henry's daughter. She never married, and was the postmistress for as long as I can remember.

The Post Office opened at nine. On mail days it was open until eight in the evening. Some people had boxes so they could get their mail whenever they wanted. The rest of the people had to get their mail from the wicket.

The mail came three times a week. It came as far as St. George's on the train. Before the trains, the mail came on the boats. Everybody knew where the boats were headed for and would give the captain or crew letters and parcels to deliver or mail.

Harold Morris, from St. George's, was the mailman for many years. He brought the mail every Monday, Wednesday and Friday. He came across in all kinds of weather – some trips were real rough. He used a horse and driving sled when the ice was heavy on the harbour. Other times in the winter he used a two-dog team and sled. When he used the dogs in heavy snow he would use snowshoes and run beside the sled. He always brought the mail.

There were times when he crossed in the boat you could not see your hand in front of you the fog was so thick.

The Telegraph Office had a cable laid across the harbour so they could hook up a telephone. It was the only phone on Sandy Point. That was really something when they got it working. They used it to receive and send messages. It made it real convenient for everybody.

Sometime between the wars the Custom's Office was moved to St. George's. The government sold the Post Office building for a house and the Post Office was moved to McFatridge's house.

The Court House

At first, the Court House was on Sandy Point, but later it was moved to St. George's. When it was on Sandy Point, the building was on the left of the government wharf.

There were two policemen. Sgt. Goodland, I think his name was William, was in charge for many years. He was a fine old man. He wouldn't hurt anything or anybody. He never had any trouble. Everybody was too busy just trying to earn enough to stay afloat – there wasn't time to get into trouble.

There was a jail for small offenses, there wasn't any robbing or killing in those days.

The circuit judge came around twice a year and the supreme court sat once a year. They came from St. John's and dealt with the few cases that warranted their judgement. Underhanded dealings in business and people who did not pay their bills were the main problems.

I can remember only one murder case. I was about ten at the time when two fellows out at Port au Port got into a fight and one killed the other. They took him away to St. John's.

20. Queen Mother Elizabeth and King George V Newfoundland stamps (issued May 12, 1938) bearing a composite "Sand[y] Point" postmark.

Barrooms

There were two saloon-type barrooms on Sandy Point. One was owned by Barter. It was just off the boardwalk to the government wharf. The other was bigger and owned by Abbotts and Shaws, if I remember correctly.

The buildings were built with nothing but the best: oak and mahogany. There were long bars with stools, tables with chairs and behind the bar a huge mirror. Brass kerosene lamps hung from the ceiling. The kind of lamps you pulled down on chains to light then raise them back in place.

Men only were admitted. You had to be 18 to get in legally. We used to get to know the bartender and get in before we should have been there. We would sit in a corner and keep quiet so only a few around us would know we were there.

They played darts, poker, cards, but mostly cards. It was great fun to be in there – all kinds of stories and jokes were being told. You could gather a lot of news there you would not hear any other place. Everybody met there – especially in the winter. When we were all out fishing or cutting wood the barrooms didn't get much business.

No food was served, just drinks. There were several kinds of beer. One Canadian beer was Black Horse from Montreal. It was five cents a bottle. There was an awful fuss when they raised it to 10 cents! They sold cigarettes like the stores. They were packed in white cardboard boxes with 100 cigarettes to a box. They sold two for a penny. We could buy rum in one- or two-gallon jugs, the old stone ones were grey with a brown top. Big glass steins were used at the bar. Draft was served in 10-inch high glasses called schooners.

There was the odd fight but not many. There were few outsiders, just the local people who went there for a good time.

Prohibition

Prohibition saw the end of the saloons. We still could get liquor off the boats that brought it in from St. Pierre & Miquelon. They came with other cargo. They brought wine in two or five gallon jugs. They also provided rum, whiskey, brandy or anything else we wanted. We could tell them what we wanted and the next time they would have it.

Prohibition also started up the local moonshiners. One of the best was Mary Halbolt. We used to go there a lot, she had three sons. We would watch her mix the ingredients and boil the mixture. The most interesting part was watching the bottles fill. As the steam forced the shine through the copper coil covered in cold water the half inch copper pipe ran steady. I think she charged 50 cents a quart.

Our local policeman, Goodland, would visit Mary and tell her that he had to raid her in a few days giving her plenty of time to take down the pipes and hide the evidence. We all thought he was a great guy and the whole thing was a lot of fun.

They never opened the barrooms after Prohibition ended. Most of the people made their own homebrew or wine by that time.

We made our homebrew in 24-gallon barrels. We bottled the beer in any and all bottles that were around. There was a use for just about every bottle that came into the house.

Making Blueberry Wine

We picked the blueberries in back of St. George's at the Dribble, that is, on the road to Steel Mountain about two miles from the government wharf. We would go over on the ferry ran by Prime Power. We would take two- or three-gallon pails. It wouldn't take long to pick them full – the berries were big and plentiful.

Once, Percy [Pieroway from St. George's] and I went in back of Flat Bay. Of course we went by boat and we took a herring barrel rigged with handles. We picked it full in a day. We always had blueberries home. We would freeze them or, if it wasn't cold enough, Mother made jam and put it up in 10-gallon wooden kegs. We had pies and puddings all winter.

To make wine, we used a molasses barrel. We put in about 12 gallons of blueberries and four gallons of molasses. Then we closed up the barrel and put in a vent – a piece of copper pipe bent so the end that would go in a bottle of water on the head of the barrel. As the wine worked, the gas bubbled out in the water so we knew when it was ready to bottle. It worked for four to six weeks depending on the temperature. When it stopped working we bottled it in anything we had. We would draw it off by syphoning it out and leaving the dregs in the bottom of the barrel.

Mothers's Hens

We always had hens, like many of the other families on Sandy
Point. Those were the best eggs – not like what we get now.

We had made a batch of blueberry wine and Freddie and I
were in a hurry so we dumped the dregs over the fence behind
the shed. We went to the store to work.

Mother always let out her hens in the morning. She had
about 30 Plymouth Rock hens and a rooster in which she took
great pride.

When we returned from work, Mother was very worried.
All her hens and the rooster were laying all over the yard. They
couldn't stand up. Couldn't even lift their heads off the
ground. She didn't know what had happened to them.

When I saw, them I guessed right away what happened.
Sure enough, they had been in the dregs. Drunk hens are a
funny sight and the proud rooster wasn't strutting his stuff –
just flopping around. They couldn't make any sort of sound
that you would recognize. Their legs were like rubber –
wobbling and swaying all over the yard.

I told Mother what I thought had happened. She wasn't
amused at all. If the hens had not got better, she threatened to
smash every bottle of wine we had. Dad got a real big kick out
of the sight. After several hours, the hens came around. I didn't
do that again. From then on I dug a hole and covered the dregs
real good. After some time had passed, Mother found it funny,
too. You couldn't see those birds without laughing. We
laughed for a long time after. Every time we had a bottle of
wine we toasted the hens.

One time Percy made a batch of blueberry wine, Charlie [his
brother] had a big ox he wanted to butcher for Hayes' Store.
We butchered it and hung it to cool. While we waited, Percy
decided to try the wine. When it came time to cut up the
carcass, they cut one hind quarter 18-pounds heavier than the
other. Gerald got a great laugh out of them and their

butchering. Everybody heard about it – stories got around fast. We loved to torment each other and that was a good chance.

[Percy, Charlie and Gerald Pieroway are brothers from St. George's.]

21. Pieroway family in front of their Sandy Point home. Back row (L-R): Mary, Howard, Harry, Joseph. Front row (L-R): Hazel, Charlie. Ethel, the other daughter, is missing from photo as she is the photographer.

Photo Album

A collection of images selected from several Sandy Point
family photo albums. Where possible, people and places have
been identified.

22. George and Mary Anne ''Polly'' (Dalton) Pieroway. Parents of George
Thomas, Alfred, Joseph Henry (Charlie's father), Susan, Johnny, William
and Martha.

23. Picnic on Sandy Point.

24. Charlie's wife, Freda Pieroway, with their daughter, Phyllis.

25. Reg and Milly Berry's house with family members in yard.

25. Elwin and Dulcie Berry in doorway of their family's home.

27. Unidentified girl in front of house.

28. Mrs. Hines' house: Mrs. Hines is standing top centre in doorway;
Frank and Trixie (Messervey) Hines (seated) and their family on left;
Gertude Parsons (centre); and Rita Messervey's children – Vera (far right)
and her brother.

29. Back row (L-R): Olive and Fred Parsons, unidentified man holding baby, Alma Hines. Front row: (L-R) Stewart Hines, Gert and Sylvia Parsons.

30. Max Berry, Freddie, Fanny, Ena, Trixie Messervey and ? child in front.

31. St. Stephen's confirmation class photo. Kay Messervey second from left, Stewart Hines and Rev. Butler at far right of front row.

32. St. Stephen's in the 1950s.

33. All that remains of St. Stephen's – its footings and graveyard (1994).

34. Phyllis Pieroway and Jean Messervey. Al Messervey looking over fence.

35. Ethel (Charlie's sister), Charlie with daughter Phyllis in front.

Rescue

Frank Forward and Roy Boyden went across to Blackbank.
They left to come home about 10 in the evening. They had a
dory rigged with a sail. Part way across a squall hit them and
turned the dory over throwing both of them in the water.

Early the next morning, at daylight, Uncle Alfred and I
were going to work on the government wharf. We could see
something bobbing on the surface about halfway across the
harbour. Some on the wharf thought it was a big log but Uncle
Alfred though we should have a look. We didn't know Frank
and Roy had not returned.

We rowed off. At first we couldn't make out what it was
but as we got closer we could see Frankie on the bottom of the
dory. We got to the dory. Uncle Alfred unwrapped a belt
Frankie had around his hand to hold him to the toepin. By that
time he was almost unconscious. He couldn't speak. He was
real cold. We asked him where Roy was. He just pointed down
with his finger.

We rowed as fast as we could for shore. There were men
there waiting. They had a stretcher to place him on. They
covered Frankie with their coats and quickly took him home.
After several days in bed, he came around. He wasn't any the
worse for the ordeal.

He told us that when he landed in the water he had been
wearing a big mackinaw coat with a belt on it. He took the belt
and wrapped it around his hand. Then he made a loop in the
other end through the buckle and slipped it over the toepin and
rolled onto the bottom of the overturned dory.

Today, he is a photographer in the United States.

Roy's body was found – they had to drag for it.

Not many men drowned from around home. One of the Chins
fell out of his boat on the way over to get a few others who had
been smelt fishing. He was standing up in his boat and a swell
knocked him overboard. They found his body on Indian Head.

Uncle Alfred drowned when he was in his early 70s. He was walking across the harbour on the ice and didn't go far enough up – the channel never froze good. He was wearing a big overcoat and had no chance. We found his body.

Doctors and a Midwife

There had been one doctor before Dr. Donald ''Dan'' Bethune.
The first had been on Sandy Point but the later ones lived in St.
George's. We had to go get them when we needed them.

Dr. Bethune came from Nova Scotia. He worked as the
dentist as well. He was a nice man. He was young when he
came to St. George's. He and Mrs. Bethune had several
children.

Dr. Bagnell came from Nova Scotia. He was young also.

Sometimes we had to go across in the worst of weather to
get the doctor. I can clearly remember having to go across and
get him. Dorothy Seward was having her first baby. There was
some sort of problem and they came and asked me to get Dr.
Bagnell. Dorothy's dad was dead and her husband was
working in Curling.

It was in the fall and heavy winds were blowing. It took
me a long time to get across the harbour. I walked to the
doctor's house and woke him. His wife made me a hot cup of
tea and then we headed back across the harbour about 2AM.

Going back was easy, the wind was behind us. The baby
was born alright. I took the doctor back in the morning. He
couldn't believe that I had crossed in the storm by myself. We
did whatever had to be done in those days – we helped
whoever needed help. We didn't think about what we were
doing, we just did it.

Elizabeth Renouf was the midwife. She borned most of the
babies on Sandy Point on her own. She had to go out at all
hours of the day and night and in all kinds of weather. Very
few babies died in birth.

Keating, the Blacksmith

He was a little man. Real short but with arms and shoulders like stovepipes. He was an old man, even when I was young. He could make anything – anchors, horseshoes, ox shoes, sleigh runners...

He had his shop out near the shore up on Lovers' Lane. It was on the harbour side near where the Forward's lived.

He had two sons, Abby and Joe, and a daughter, Annie. They were Irish Roman Catholics. We spent a lot of time with him from the time I was small. Our families were life long friends. They were a real nice family.

As kids, we loved to watch the sparks fly. He worked real fast. He could make axes in no time at all. Ploughs took more time. He had nothing to go by except what was in his head.

The bellows were big: six-feet long and three-feet deep. He kept the handle tucked under his arm. Sometimes he would let us pump for him, as long as we didn't pump too hard. He was real good natured. Never saw him get mad at anybody. He smoked a crooked pipe. We loved to go to the store and get his tobacco for him. We would do anything he wanted.

He was kept busy as there was always things breaking and new things to be made. He was an important part of the community. Everybody depended on him. He did good work.

36. Several blacksmith-made tools.

Building Houses

Houses were built in the fall when fishing was slack. Almost everybody built a two-storey house. Everybody who could would pitch in and help build the house. Some years there would be several to build, so the work had to get done fast before bad weather set in.

Even if a couple got married in the spring they lived with relatives until the fall. Then their house would be built. Nobody could take time off during fishing. That was the only way to make money for most of the people on Sandy Point and all around the harbour.

Hubert White was the mason. He lived in St. George's. He was a fine old man. He built all the chimneys and fireplaces around the area. The quarried stone and brick came in by schooner. The stone was cut about two-feet long by 12-inches wide. It was interesting to watch him build fireplaces. He mixed all his own mortar. Nobody could help him with that. That was too important to leave to anybody else. He was usually paid by the day. He worked real steady and was always busy. He was the only one around who did that kind of work.

As kids, we had lot of interesting people to watch at their work. We were so happy when they wanted us to do something for them.

I don't ever remember seeing a house burn. Everybody took real good care. They cleaned the chimneys regularly and took special care of the stoves.

Dry Well Drilling

Whenever anybody needed a well they would buy the drill points and pipe. The drill point was two-feet long by two-inches in diameter. It had a metal outer case with holes in it and inside was a fine mesh screen with a three-inch tapered point.

We would bore a hole in the floor of the house. Our's was in the pantry. To start the bit in the sand, we would place a hardwood plank on the pipe and hit it with an eight-pound hammer. Then we would screw on a length of pipe six-feet long. From then on, we would pound the pipe further down in the sand and keep adding lengths of pipe until we figured we were down deep enough. Our well was down 18-feet.

When we got it deep enough we put a standpipe on it up to the countertop height and then placed the pump on the pipe. The first five or six gallons would be grouty, then it would clear up. We never ran out of water.

We didn't have any problems driving wells on Sandy Point, but they didn't have it so easy in St. George's.

37. Ada Swyer's home. A typical Sandy Point house.

Floating Houses

Whenever a building had to be moved across the harbour it would be jacked up and placed on rollers. Then we would haul it with block-and-tackle. It was strictly a manpower operation but sometimes we used a horse to take up the slack while moving the building to the shore.

We used logs that were longer than the house. There was a pile of logs anybody could use as they needed them. They would use them and then bring them back and haul them up to dry again. The raft of cross-piled logs would be ready, they would be prepared before the moving day.

The building would be moved onto the logs. Oil drums were then strapped in place all around the building. Tar barrels were sometimes used. Usually two boats would tow the building – one boat on each corner. It would take one and a half to two hours to cross the harbour. A very calm day was needed for this operation.

The buildings would be landed in the shore near the railway station on the St. George's side. It was fairly easy to move houses on Sandy Point as it was so flat. When they got across the harbour it was a different story. It was a hard haul to get some of them in place in St. George's.

That was real hard work. Most of the time, things went well. If the wind came up while the tow was under way it got real tricky, especially if the building was high.

Some buildings were hauled across on the thick winter ice.

Mill Work

I worked for two summers at Tucker & Co. Mill at the mouth of Barachois Brook. I cut lathes for lobster pots and plaster work. I was 18, my first summer there.

I stayed at Lil McLean's and went home on Sundays. I worked six days every week. We worked from seven in the morning until six, with one hour off for dinner. We were fed at the cookshack and the food was good. I was paid about three dollars a day. That sure was good money then.

The weather didn't bother us as it was a big mill all under cover. The mill was on the east side of the river mouth.

We fished herring in the spring. Dad fished salmon while I worked at the mill.

When the mill closed in the fall, we set trawl.

38. Joseph Henry Pieroway's key ring.

Working With Wood

Barrel Marking

When I was real young, we didn't have any special equipment to made barrels. We made 150 to 170 every winter along about February. We didn't have a stave saw so we had to cut the fir in September up Main River.

We would stay there and cut for two or three days. We would go to the sandbar in the river and anchor behind the bar for protection. We had to cut the trees and carry them back to the shore and load them in the boat.

When we got them to Sandy Point, we cut them about 35-inches long. Then we would split the pieces and shape each stave out with a drawknife. Each stave started about an inch thick, we shaved it down to three-quarters of an inch.

The hoops were cut from one-inch birch. We cut the trees and split them lengthwise. The strips of birch were cut off with the drawknife to form the hoop. We used a [work]horse made of a log with four legs. There was a cleat head to hold the birch in place. Then we would bend the strip over the round log and secure it to form the hoop. Later, when we were able to get iron hoops, we still used birch for the belly of the barrels and iron hoops on the shim.

Millage Messervey and Reg Berry got a stave saw – that saved us lots of time. Butt's Mill cut staves. They had a head maker, too.

We made the heads out of pine. We cut very large logs for the heads – big around. They were then junked about 18-inches long and split into inch-thick pieces. The head was made of two or three pieces put together with dowels and then planed off. With a drawknife we would shape the head. Using a compass we would scribe an 18-inch circle. Then we had to saw to the mark. With the knife, we tapered it back half way on each side to fit tight.

We made half-barrels for shipping our salmon. We always salted our own salmon for use at home – that was the only way we could keep them.

Boats

Jim Parsons, Alfred Renouf and Fred Hines were the boat builders. They would build boats themselves or help anyone who needed them.

They built many St. George's punts – a unique local motor boat – and dories.

Fred Hines helped us build our last boat. We built it on the hill in our yard behind the house. We cut the spruce for the timbers and dug the roots out for the knees. The keel and stern post stem were cut from witch hazel, white spruce for the gunnel. We could bend white spruce anyway we needed. It finished up real smooth. The planks were cut from pine. All the logs except the pine were cut up Main River. The pine came from up Barachois Brook. The inside timbers were juniper.

The pine trees were 80 to 90 feet high – what beautiful cutting. Sam Butt sawed the plank and timbers for the boat. We didn't have a mill until I was about 20. We had a pit saw out back of the barn, that was slow hard work.

The keel was 22-feet long. Finished she was 20-feet overall topside. We painted her green with a white stripe.

When our boat was ready to launch, we used rollers to move it. All the men got together and pulled it along Lovers' Lane, past Forward's, to the shore.

There was always lots of help around whenever we needed to pull our boat out of the water. We just had to pass the word around and they were there. We helped everybody else when they needed us.

We had two sails and a jib in the boat. When it was calm we had to row, the sweeps (oars) were about 12-feet long. Our first motor was a four-horsepower Acadia from Bridgewater, Nova Scotia. First it came by schooner to Halifax and then to

Sandy Point on another schooner. There were about 200 boats at the peak of the fishing. They certainly could make a wonderful sound on a calm morning when everybody was heading out. There isn't another sound I can remember that I like as much as those make n' brakes. Not everybody liked the engines – some liked the old way better. Some old people thought these engines were the work of the devil.

Every spring, in March, we scraped our boats and painted the bottom with copper paint to stop the worms – it was reddish in colour – up to the waterline.

We sold the boat to Delphus LaSaga. One time when we were home, we tried to find it. Percy had seen it in Stephenville, but we couldn't find it, I would have liked to see the old boat again.

One of the boatbuilders built a small schooner, about 20 feet long, and called her *Bluenose*. We all had a good laugh out of his choice of a name. She had the same lines as the real schooner. The boatbuilders could build anything. We spent a lot of time around where anything was being built.

Coffins

Jim Parsons built coffins as well as boats. Whenever one was needed, he would make whatever size was required. When the folks died their measurements were taken and Jim would build the coffin out of pine. He lined them and covered the outside with a purple fabric trimmed with white.

Jim was almost stone deaf. We used to like watching his wife talk to him using sign language. We were bad at times, we would make lots of noise and yell just to see if he could hear.

He chewed tobacco all the time. Whenever we got in his way, he would never say anything – just spit tobacco at us. He worked so fast it was fun to watch him.

We all liked both Jim and his wife, Aunt Polly. She was almost blind. They had one son, he went overseas to the first World War and never returned. I don't remember where he died but it was real hard on them.

They lived across from the school. If we needed a drink of water we went to their house. Sometimes 25 of us would all go over to see Aunt Polly at recess time. She would make cookies and ginger breads and give them to us. She was a very small woman and could barely see to get around. It was marvellous how she could do so much.

We would saw wood and split it for them and shovel snow in the winter. Often five or six of us would go together to help them. They were getting well along in years so we liked to help them.

Dogs and Wood Cutting

We had two dogs most of the time. They were mixed breeds –
big and good-natured but strong. One favourite was Lad. He
was almost as big as a Newfoundland dog but white and brown
in colour. We got him as a pup in the spring and he grew real
fast all summer.

By Christmas time, Dad figured it was time to train him.
We took him to the fish shed where we kept the sled. Dad put
Lad in the harness and the dog took off for home as proud as
he could be. If we held the collar, he would jump to get in it –
then you had to be ready to jump on the sled. He got so quick
we had to tie the sled to the shed then put him in the collar. We
would never catch the sled if he took off. We had to be ready
to untie the sled fast. The dog seemed to love to work.

A lot of the work we did was heavy so we had two dogs.
We made a body harness with a collar and snap hooks for each
dog.

In March, Dad and I would go to Main River and cut our
next winter's hardwood. We used 16-20 cords a year. We
would stay about two weeks. Dad cut everything with an axe
and I would haul the logs out with the dogs. We piled them on
the bank of the river.

We would come back in the summer and take it to Sandy
Point by the boatload. Nobody ever took the wood. We all got
our wood the same way.

I would go back in the summer – leaving home about
three or four o'clock in the morning. I could load the boat with
about two cord of wood. I had stakes for the sides so I could
pile it about two feet above the gunnel.

I used a horse and cart to get it from the wharf to the
house. When we got it home we would stand it up to dry. We
didn't have a horse but Uncle Alfred and Charlie Parsons did.
We borrowed the horse whenever we needed it. There was no
need of everybody having everything. All we had to do was
ask.

Gordie Parsons often helped me haul the wood home. We would cut it up later in the summer or early fall. It took a lot of work to have enough wood on hand to keep us warm and cook all the food. It was easy cutting then – lots of good wood around for everybody.

Driving Logs on Flat Bay Brook

We worked for Ron Baxter of Baxter Enterprises from St. John's. They owned a mill at Muddy Hole at the mouth of Flat Bay Brook.

We would go in behind St. George's and cut pine in January, February and March. We cut the logs and John Butler twitched them out with the horse. It was about a mile and a half haul. There they would be piled on the bank of the river.

When the ice went out the end of April or early May the drive would begin.

The crew numbered from 20 to 25 on the drive. I worked in the forward boats on some drives. They were big dories, 20-feet long and real high on the sides. We would keep the logs moving so they would not pile up or cause a jam. When the logs got piled up, it was hard work to get the drive moving again. Nobody got hurt but we often got wet. It was real cold in the water in May.

When it was time to camp for the night, we would let the logs jam. Then break them loose again in the morning. There was another crew to set up camp and prepare the food. There was always lots of good hot meals. We sure could eat when we were driving.

We often had about two miles of river full of big pine logs. We wore spiked boots and used peavees and pike poles to work the logs. The pike poles were from 10- to 15-feet long. Some men could move over the logs like they were dancing. They were always trying to see who could go the furthest the fastest, or roll a log the longest. I liked the drives – they were a lot of fun as well as hard work.

I was on the drive the day you [Phyllis] were born. We were coming down and, about four miles above the bridge, we stopped for several hours to fight a forest fire. When we got to the camp that night, I got word that you were born. I walked into St. George's to see you and your mother. I walked back to Flat Bay later that night.

We finished the drive the next day. We had a boom across the mouth of the river to hold the logs. It was hard work, but I always enjoyed being with the crew.

38. Loading pulp wood on the *Convallaria* at anchor in St. George's Bay.

Berry Picking

Different kinds of berries grew in various spots around the
harbour and on Sandy Point. Everybody picked berries to make
their jams and jellies as well as put them down for cooking.

Partridge berries grew on the marsh at Black Bank and
Bank Head – above Flat Bay.

We could always find cranberries at Flat Bay. One fall
Dad and I went to Flat Bay after a wind and rain storm had
passed. The marshes were flooded – all the cranberries had
floated to the surface. All we had to do was scoop them up.
They were even cleaned. We filled five boxes the easy way.
They were easy to pick anyway because they were so big.

Raspberries grew on Whale, Burnine and Jaunters Islands.
They would make real good jam. Mother always had a good
supply by wintertime.

Marshberries are like cranberries but sort of grey in
colour. They were very good. They grew on Sandy Point in the
wet areas.

Maidenberries grew on Sandy Point. They were white and
about the size of a pea. They grew on runners. We picked them
late in the summer or early fall. They made delicious jam.

Bakeapples grew in back of Shallop Cove. The whole
marsh would be yellow in the summer. We picked them in
August. Once, Dad and I had gone to Seal Cove for hay and
the wind picked up. We couldn't take the hay across the
harbour so we went towards Indian Head. We picked two
biscuit boxes full of bakeapples in no time at all. The berries
were big and golden – perfect for picking.

Wild strawberries grew in lots of places around the
harbour. On Sandy Point, they grew along the beaches and the
area towards The Opening. In the summer we would take our
salmon nets up towards The Opening to clean them. Mother
would bring our lunch up to us. She would pick berries until
we were ready to go back. Then she would come back in the

boat with us. There was always lots of berries up there. Wild strawberries are so good with fresh cream.

Gooseberries grew wild up on Burnine Island. The bushes would be bent over when they were ripe. Mom always made jam. I especially like gooseberry.

Everybody picked berries – the women and girls picked a lot. The men and boys helped whenever they had time. It took a lot to keep us going all winter. Everybody had to help but nobody minded because they were so good.

40. Mary Lorraine (Parsons) Pieroway, Charlie's mother. (1919)

Rabbit Catching

In the winter we would go to Bottom Brook or up Flat Bay
Brook for six or seven days at a time. We had a big white
cotton tent to live in.

To set up we would clear an area in the snow and pitch the
tent – piling snow around the bottom of the tent. Then we put
up a frame of small poles over the tent and covered it with fir
boughs. We piled them on real thick.

The stove was set up in the middle with the pipe through
the roof. The stove was about two-feet long, a foot wide and
just over a foot high. We had to keep it going all the time.
Sometimes there was too much heat – we'd have to go outside.

We cut more fir boughs and piled them on the floor. On
top of that we spread a piece of canvas to sleep on. We didn't
have sleeping bags then – didn't even use blankets. We wore
wool everything – from the longjohns out.

We each had two dogs and a komtic and a gun. The gun
was used for partridge or, if we were real lucky, to kill a
moose. We couldn't afford to waste ammunition on rabbits.
We got all we needed in the snares. Usually we took 60 to 70
rabbits home after the week. They stayed frozen. When the
weather turned mild, we would bottle or can what was left.

Hunting Geese

Usually in March, when the ice was breaking up, three or four
of us would to go goose hunting. We would take our dog teams
to Mattis Point above Main Gut bridge. The channel there
never freezes because the current is too strong.

We would borrow a dory from someone there. We set up
camp on the shore. Then one of us would row the other two off
to the ice. We called the pieces of ice pans or clumps. Some
were piled high. That was what we wanted so we could be
above the geese on shore.

We wore white canvas suits over our regular clothes. We
made the suits ourselves. The canvas was sorta heavy so we
stitched them by hand. Nothing fancy. But using a palm needle
we got them together. There was a hood, too. And with white
wool gloves we were well-camouflaged. The gloves were more
like mitts. They were knit with one finger and a thumb.

We used two double-barrelled guns. One beside us and the
other ready. When we started shooting, the geese would take to
the air so we had to be fast. Most of the time we would get two
geese each with the two guns.

We would each get on a floating clump and let the tide
carry us down among the geese. We aimed for the wings, if we
didn't get them the first time they could not get away.

The third fellow in the dory, who had rowed off, would
pick us up and row to the flats where we would pick up the
geese. We would take turns shooting and rowing.

We would stay two or three days. We cleaned the geese
and hung them. They were fat and plump – real good eating. It
was a lot of work to get there so the older men didn't bother. It
was fun for us then. We would give geese to the old people
who could not get their own.

We took molasses buns, cooked corned beef, lots of tea
and anything else we didn't have to cook.

Charlie Goodland, Freddie Messervey, Morgan Messervey
and I usually went together. The fresh meat was a treat at that

time of year. If we didn't get a moose or caribou, the only other fresh meat we had all winter was rabbit.

We waited for calm weather before we would go but it was always cold. We would boil the kettle and have tea and buns – then we would forget about the cold. We always had a good time there.

Getting Cows

We always had a cow. If she had a heifer we would keep it but if the calf was a steer we butchered it.

When we had to buy a cow from the farmers around the harbour, we would go across to St. George's and walk around the harbour through the Crossing to Stephenville then to the Cape. We didn't mind walking. We would walk the animal back to St. George's and load the animal in our boat and land it on Sandy Point. It would take a full day to go and get a cow. A long day at that.

Once, Dad and I went out to Kippen's to buy a cow. It was real calm so we decided to bring her back in the boat instead of walking her back. The farm was right by the shore. The farmer had three cows. We picked the one we wanted, a big brown and white one. We had a bit to eat with the farmer and his wife. The farmer's wife gave us the milk she had milked from the cow in the morning. The farmer didn't think much of us taking the cow in the boat.

41. A cow in back of the Pieroway family house.

I ran the boat alongside in as close as I could to the shore. They loaded the cow by using big poles laid from the shore. She walked right out as they led her. We tied her head, around the horns, to the forward thwart. We put another rope across her back and lashed it to the gunnel. She stayed real calm and we didn't have any trouble. We hauled up near the sand beach and she jumped out and I led her home. It had to be very calm to do that. She was a real good milker.

We would walk around the harbour to get a beef to butcher. Warren Parsons and I walked to the Cape once and brought a beef back. There was no other way to get them there – everybody did it that way.

Getting Hay

We had lots of hay on Sandy Point but we also cut some in Seal Cove on the Holly place. When it was ready to bring home we would cut poles and jam them in the gunnel. Then we would nail more poles the other way to make a rack on the boat. We would load the hay and tramp it down hard. It would be piled high over our heads going across. We needed fine weather to get across the harbour with a full load of hay.

We stored our hay in the loft of the fish shed. Our shed was about 45-feet by 30-feet with a high peaked roof so we could store a lot of stuff in there.

We kept sheep too. We would kill off three or four each fall. We had an ice house. That is where we hung the carcases. They stayed frozen in there. The ice house was 12-feet by 16-feet with a sawdust floor at least a foot thick.

The ice was cut every spring in March and piled to the roof. We covered it with sawdust. We used out of it all summer to pack our salmon in for shipment.

42. Taking a break while haying. (L-R) Gus Forward, Elwin Berry, Rex Messervey, Charlie Messervey, Leslie Berry and Freddie Messervey.

Using Hides and Skins

We never bought leather. Whenever we butchered a steer or cow we nailed the skin on the end of the shed. It was nailed up good and tight to keep its shape. When it was dry, we would take it down and cut it in strips. They were usually one-foot wide and 30-inches long, or whatever size moccasins we wanted to make.

We scraped the strips with a piece of glass to take off all the hair. We boiled juniper and spruce bark to make the tan. The strips would be left in the tan for about two weeks. The leather would be real brown when we took the pieces out of the kettle. The skin would plim up and be nice and thick, real soft also, and easy to work with.

Before cutting, we would hand-rub the strips to break up the fiber. We also put oil on the skins after they were rubbed – we used porpoise oil.

We had our patterns or, if we wanted something different, we made new patterns. We cut the leather and sewed the pieces together by hand.

Cow hides were used for the shoe part and the leggings were made of calf or seal skins. The best skins of all were caribou.

The moccasins were made round-style without laces. We had to sew gut over the top to form a case to pull a drawstring through. They tied just under the knee. They were real warm and comfortable.

Sheep skins were used to make mitts, caps and slippers. The wool was placed on the inside with the leather out. The wool was clipped short – about one-half-inch to an inch was left. The skins were washed, then bleached in lye. They would come out real white. Lamb skin was the best for caps as it was very soft. Lamb skin was not strong enough for mitts or slippers. The caps were made to come right down over the neck and ears, almost down to the chin. They tied under the chin, they were wonderfully warm. The winters were long and cold. We spent a lot of time out of doors so we needed clothes to keep warm and dry. Only our eyes were left uncovered.

43. Cobbler's lasts.

Cobblers

Jack Young (Coady) and his family lived by themselves, away from everybody else in the upper end of Sandy Point. They always had a real good garden. We used to go there a lot because Jack was known for his storytelling. We never believed the tall tales but we liked to listen. He repaired shoes and boots. He also made moccasins.

Oliver Alexander lived by himself in a small house near the Renouf's. He was crippled. He had a real bad limp. We used to torment him a lot.

The LeRoux girls had a tame seagull they kept in a cage. Freddie Messervey, Leroux Parsons, Jack Guy and I took the gull. We knocked on Oliver's door. When he opened it, we threw the gull inside. What a racket! Oliver tried to chase the gull out – it was flying around inside his small house. When he finally got it out, we caught the gull, and put it back in its cage. The next day Freddie and I went to see Oliver and he told us all about the terrible prank. He was so startled he didn't know who had been at the door. We would have been in a lot of trouble if anybody had found out we did it. We knew it was wrong but we thought it was funny at the time.

Oliver repaired anything made of leather – shoes, boots, horse harness, he put soles on shoes, made moccasins, repaired coats. We would buy sealskin Eskimo [Innuit] moccasins and get Oliver to put leather soles on them – they sure were nice to walk in. He did wonderful work. He was always busy. Shoes and boots were expensive so it was necessary to keep them in good repair.

Porpoises and Whales

We kept a gallon jar of porpoise oil all the time. We used it to rub in leather and to keep machines running smooth. There were plenty of porpoise around when I was young. We would shoot one. Sometimes we only needed half so we would share the kill. We never took more than we needed. Some people ate the meat – I couldn't – they were so nice to watch swimming.

Sometimes they would get in the nets and die – then we didn't have to kill them.

We would skin the porpoise. Its fat was real white and all over the inside about an inch thick. We would cut up the skin in small pieces and render it out in a big pot over a fire out of doors. It didn't smell bad and came out clear. I hated to kill them but we needed the oil.

The porpoise were so much fun to watch. Sometimes there would be hundreds of them in the harbour. We used to sit on the government wharf and watch them in the evening when the waters were calm that was a pretty sight.

Some would get rolled up in the salmon nets. If they were still alive we let them go after we got them out.

There were always whales around. Especially in the spring when the big run of herring was on. There were not as many in the fall but there was always some around. Some would run ashore. Then we would have to get a gang together and tow it off to deep water and sink it. We couldn't leave the whale there to rot. They sure smelled bad. We would take them way outside the harbour. They may have washed up somewhere else – we didn't care, as long as it wasn't where we had to smell it for months. We never used the whales for anything. They were a big nuisance.

Once, Dad and I were on the way back up the harbour just off the lighthouse and a whale came up so close we could have touched it if we had leaned over. It blew. Nobody was scared of them but that one startled us.

I don't remember any boats being damaged by whales but they ruined many nets. That was real bad because we would have to take the nets out and repair them if there was enough left to save. Catching fish was so important when the run was on we had to get all we could as fast as possible. To have a whale ruin a net was real costly.

On the *Humorist*

Dad and I both sailed on the *Humorist*. She was three-masted but didn't have a bowspit or topmast. The builders made a mistake when they were building her. The forward section was much higher than it was supposed to be. She was built in Trinity Bay. She turned up at the bow a lot more than others like her. She also had engines for power when we needed it – you couldn't always depend on the wind.

The crew was mostly from Greenspond, Bonavista Bay. The engineer was from St. John's. The cook was Bob Humphrey. He was a crippled fellow who was real strong on the Salvation Army. They were a real good bunch. Captain Dominy was a real good man to work for.

On my second trip on her, the engineer's brother left the crew. The engineer made me his second. I liked that a lot because I didn't have to stand any watch on deck. I just had to sit in a big easychair in the warm engine room below and watch the engines.

I made many trips on her. We would go to Norfolk, Virginia with a load of fish and bring back drums of gasoline.

On one trip, we had gone into a port in North Carolina and unloaded. There, we picked up a charter to take wicker baskets of nuts off a wrecked ship. That was in August or September – we ate nuts for months after. We took a lot home. That was a real treat for everybody.

It was interesting going ashore in the southern States. We got to see all sorts of things that didn't grow in our part of the world. We were real happy some of the snakes we saw there didn't live in Newfoundland. They sure were big. The spiders were huge, too. They used to hide in the bunches of bananas and grapes. We had to be careful when we took supplies on board. We didn't want them loose inside the ship.

We also went down north to October Harbour in Labrador. We would trade flour, tobacco, flannelette, bright-coloured cottons and beads for furs. What glorious pelts they would have. They were always happy to see us, real friendly people. We would have a good load of furs on board on the way back. That was nice cargo to handle.

We used to go to the Grey Islands [off Conche, on the east side of the Northern Peninsula] at the start of the summer fishing. We would go to St. John's and pick up the families of the men on the fishing boats and take them to the islands. We took the families back to St. John's for the winter. It was a rugged island but it was infested with rabbits.

There wasn't any harbour [on the Grey Islands]. We had to back in against the cliff and anchor. We would hold there by attaching ropes to the cliff hooks. We had to watch the weather real carefully. We would have to get out of there fast if the wind came up. We would have been splinters smashed against the cliffs.

It was tricky for the women and little children with all their things to get on the island and just as dangerous getting off again. A lot of people spent the summer months on the off islands as the men fished.

Captain Dominy was a marvellous man with a boat. Once we had to put into LaScie to get out of a storm. The harbour entrance isn't very wide – with cliffs all around. We got in alright and anchored for the night. From where we were anchored, the next morning we couldn't see how he got in there. It looked like there were cliffs all around the harbour. We couldn't see the entrance but the captain knew the coast. It made you feel good knowing you were with somebody who knew the coast like that.

Making for Seldom Come By

Another time on the *Humorist,* we were over on the east coast and a snowstorm came up. The storm went around from southeast to northwest. Captain Dominy decided to make a run for Seldom Come By on Fogo.

We met a big two-masted American schooner outside. They asked if they could follow us in. The *Humorist* was under power but the American was under sail. Father climbed the mast and turned the lamp around so the other schooner could see to follow very close.

She was under sail with a bone in her teeth. The *Humorist* came in close by another schooner and anchored. The big American schooner couldn't get her sails down fast enough and they ran aground on a bar. They probably would have landed on shore if the bar had not been there.

There was 16 other boats in the small harbour. That was a dangerous storm. We couldn't last outside.

Two days later, when the storm died down, several of the schooners that had engines towed the American schooner off the bar. The captain was most high in his praise of Captain Dominy. He never would have made it without us leading the way in. He didn't know the coast.

Three small two-masted coastal schooners were caught in the storm. They lost most of their canvas and ended up over off Scotland. They were driven ahead of the storm all the way across the Atlantic. I'm glad I wasn't on any of them.

Schr: "Humorist"
Reg. No: 143006
Built: 1921 (Reg. 18 Aug. 1921)
Built by: Josiah Frampton, Monroe, Trinity Bay, Nfld.
Length: 111'6''   Breadth: 26'6''   Depth: 12'6''
Reg. tons: 140.57   Signal Letters
Gross tons: –   Top flag: T
Master: 2nd flag: C
                     3rd flag: S
                     Bottom flag: W
Owners: Henry W. Stone of Monroe, Trinity Bay, Nfld.,
Merchant, 64 shares.
Transactions:
Henry W. Stone sold 48 shares to Walter S. Monroe of St.
John's, Nfld., on 31 May 1923.
Registry closed March 1, 1929; vessel registered anew due
to alterations of tonnage.

> *St. John's Shipping Register* – Reel #C 4851
> Fisheries Museum of the Atlantic, Lunenburg, N.S.

From the *Log of the IGA Marine Railway* which operated at
St. Anthony from 1928-75:
Schooner *Humorist* – Capt. Dominy, master; Monroe
Exports, St. John's, owners. Docked Sept. 14, 1932,
released Sept. 16, 1932. Weight 172 tons; bottom cleaned
and painted. Charged $81.54.

> *The Grenfell Dock.* Francis Patey (Bebb Publishing Ltd.)

"Captain John Dominy was her master at the time of her
loss ... She struck the land at Point Roche near Argentia.
Her crew escaped ... Six casks of fish and much of her gear
were salvaged. And that was Christmas 1933."

> *Newfoundland Ships and Men.* Andrew Horwood
> (Macy's Publishing)

Building Our Windmill

We built our windmill in 1940. We had to take down a shed so we could put the stand near the house. The stand was made out of heavy timbers. The four corner posts were 25-feet high. We bought the frame for the generator and the fan blades. There were two blades on the windmill.

We lifted all the parts to the top of the stand by ropes. As usual, there was lots of hands around to help.

We ran wires down the stand and into the house to connect to the two batteries. We ran a radio and five lights. The lights were in the kitchen, back kitchen, pantry, front room, and Mother's bedroom. They were all on the ground floor. We used 12 watt bulbs, they weren't very bright but they were better than using lamps all the time.

We shut the windmill off at night. There was a brake on it to stop the blades from turning. The brake was a 25-pound weight.

We still used kerosene lamps but it was nice to have the lights. There was always a spell in the summer when there was very little wind so we couldn't generate power.

44. The Pieroway house showing windmill stand on the left side.

I worked with the crews building the American base, Harmon Field, in Stephenville. The men working there didn't have to go in the Services. They considered the construction of the American bases real important.

Once the base was built, it was never the same around home. There were so many big planes on the go all the time. All that noise was hard for the people to get used to. The loudest sound we had heard before was the engines in some of the coastal boats or a lot of fishing boats going out together. The make n' breaks sure sounded better than those bombers.

Having a radio was wonderful. It didn't matter how scratchy the sound was, we listened to everything. Getting the news during war time was very important. Most of the families had someone fighting overseas – some were in the British services and others in the Canadian. With all the troubles of war around, we especially enjoyed the music.

About the Author

Phyllis Pieroway was born in St. George's, Newfoundland and lived on Sandy Point. With her parents she moved to Curling, near Corner Brook, and later immigrated to Canada.

Halifax and, later, the Dartmouth-area became home. Cole Harbour and Dartmouth schools consumed her childhood years. Many summers were spent in St. George's.

Photography has always been an interest. A grade six graduation present of a camera set Phyllis on a visual path. A Life Member of the Photographic Guild of Nova Scotia, her photography has earned awards and acceptances in national and international salons. Images have been published in *Photo Life* and *Canadian Geographic* magazines, and on postcards, calendars, brochures, government and travel publications.

Phyllis married Wendell Blades. They have three children: Joe, Carol and Ruth. Dartmouth, Nova Scotia is still home base for her travel, photography and writing.

Other Titles of Interest

Acorn, Milton. *Reading from* **More Poems for People**. 0-919957-62-5 (cassette) STE $9.95 *
Beutel (ed & cartoons). *True (Blue) Grit: A Frank McKenna Review in Cartoons and Essays.*
0-921411-53-7. MAPP $16.95 *
Blades, Joe. *Cover Makes a Set.* 0-919957-60-9. STE $8.95 *
Blades, Joe. *future now past.* 0-919957-61-7. STE $3.95
Blades, Joe, *Stones of My Flesh,* 0-919957-64-1. STE $2.95
Bull, Arthur; Bull, Ruth (ill.) *Hawthorn,* 0-921411-24-3. BJP $4.95
Deahl, James. *Under The Watchful Eye: Poetry and Discourse.* 0-921411-30-8 BJP $11.95 *
Deahl, James; *Under The Watchful Eye: Book and Video Set.* (incl. 0-921411-30-8,
SF-93-501) 0-921411-31-6 BJP $34.95 *
Deahl, James; Fitzgerald, D.C. *Poetry and music from Under The Watchful Eye* (cassette)
0-921411-32-4, BJP $11.95 *
flaming, p.j. *voir dire.* 0-921411-26-X. New Muse 1994. BJP $11.95 *
Folsom, Eric. *Poems for Little Cataraqui.* 0-921411-28-6. BJP $10.95 *
Footman, Jennifer (ed) *An Invisible Accordion: A Canadian Poetry Association Anthology,*
0-921411-38-3, BJP $14.95 *
Footman, Jennifer *St Valentine's Day,* 0-921411-45-6, BJP $13.95 *
Gibbs, Robert. *Earth Aches,* 0-921411-36-7, BJP $2.95
Grace, Mary Elizabeth; Shin, Ann (eds). *Crossroads Cant: spoken word word as art song
word.* 0-921411-48-0. BJP $13.95 *
Hawkes, Robert. *This Grievous Injury.* 0-921411-41-3. BJP $2.95
LeDuc, M.R., *Reflections of a Frog.* 0-921411-40-5. BJP $3.95
mclennan, rob *Poems from the Blue Horizon.* 0-921411-34-0. BJP $3.95
Pieroway, Charles Warren. *Sandy Point Map.* 0-921411-46-4. MAPP $4.95 *
Pieroway, Phyllis. *Memories of Sandy Point, St George's Bay, Newfoundland.* 0-921411-33-2.
MAPP $14.95 *
Redekopp, Jean. *A View from the Bucket.* 0-921411-52-9. MAPP $14.95 *
Richards, David Adams. *A Lad from Brantford & other essays,* 0-921411-25-1. BJP $11.95 *
Schmidt, Tom. *The Best Lack All.* New Muse 1995. 0-921411-37-5. BJP $12.95 *
Smith, Diana. *Ripples from the Phoenix.* 0-921411-29-4. MAPP $2.95
Trakl, Georg; Skelton, Robin (translator) *Dark Seasons.* 0-921411-22-7. BJP $10.95 *
Vaughan, R.M. *The InCorrupt Tables.* 0-921411-44-8. BJP $2.95
Wendt, Karl. *Chaste Wood.* 0-921411-11-1. BJP $7.95 *

Ask your favourite bookstore to order these books (from General Distribution Services in Canada and the USA). Or order direct from us: individual orders must be prepaid and must include postage (in Canada: $2 for first * book + $1 each additional book, $0.75 per all other chapbook titles) and all Canadian orders must add 7% GST on the total books and postage (GST 12489 7943 RT****). All orders from individuals must be prepaid by cheque or money order. No credit card orders. No cash via post, please.

Order from:
M·A·P·PRODUCTIONS
BOX 596 STN A   Ph   506 454-5127
FREDERICTON NB E3B 5A6   Fax 506 454-5127
CANADA   E·mail jblades@nbnet.nb.ca